MW00935224

Facing the Giant

between a rock and a heart place

by: TERRY W. BOMAR

ISBN-10:1497472598
ISBN-13:9781497472594

DEDICATION

This book is lovingly dedicated to my beautiful mother

Violet June Bomar

June 10, 1923 – April 8, 1982

A perfect example of a Godly and virtuous woman

Proverbs 31:10-31
Who can find a virtuous woman?
for her price is far above rubies.

CONTENTS

ACKNOWLEDGMENTS

I want to thank all my friends that have always supported my ministry and encouraged me to write this book.

I also want to thanks my brothers and sisters:
Sheila, Ken, Sheryl and Keith

for all the wonderful family times.

Our lives together have continuously been filled with laughter, love, support and truth.

Chapter 1

The Stand-Off

My mother was standing in her bedroom fighting back tears facing a giant that was ripping her heart out - that giant was me!

Mom was a middle-aged divorced mother of five children; two girls and three boys. By working two or three jobs at a time, she had successfully raised the first three kids and had two teenage boys to go. For us, it was a  great single-parent family that she had every right to proud of, because she had done a marvelous job. She had provided a financially stable home with a warm loving atmosphere. But most importantly, she conscientiously instilled a bedrock of character and values in each of her children that was the foundation of her family. It was a wonderful loving home ...then all hell broke loose and she was no match for the monster that emerged.

A giant was born on the railroad tracks that I used for a short-cut to walk home from school. I was only thirteen years old, walking the rails with a friend of mine when he challenged me to try *"one little pill,"* half the size of a baby aspirin. When I refused, he took out a razor-blade and cut the little pill into eight tiny pieces. He licked his finger and daubed up one of the orange slivers and said, "this teeny weeny little thing isn't going to hurt you."

But it did, ...it changed everything.

The giant grew slowly at first, but over the next couple of years it changed my set of friends, my thoughts, my choices, my habits, my priorities and my personality.

For a long time I kept the titan well hidden behind the polite courteous manners that my mother had taught us. I successfully lived a double life with good grades in school during the week - and drugs, crime and chaos on the weekends. But just as a cute little lion cub grows into a ravenous beast, I grew into a selfish voracious animal that only cared about me and my reputation with friends.

Mom had been as good as any mother could be; but I still chose to follow my own destructive lifestyle, regardless of the consequences. In three short years I had stripped away all the peace in our family and replaced it with selfish fits of profanity, rage and rebellion. I don't like to think about the times mom had to call the police on me or how many nights I heard my mother crying herself to sleep. All of her pride and plans for my life had turned into extreme disappointment and relentless worry. I'll never forget the look she had staring in disbelief, the night I stood in the doorway screaming at her: *"I'm on LSD right now! What are you going to do about it?"*

The little boy she loved to call her *"little man"* had transformed into her own personal Goliath ...and now she was locked in a *"Stand-off!"*

My mother's story is just one among millions of parents that spend endless nights of confusion terrified of what's happening to their children. Maybe you're one of those parents, wringing your hands wondering what you did wrong, and praying that someone somewhere will step in with a miracle. Or perhaps your adversary is totally different ...rebellious teens aren't the only giants that can turn success into a stand-off – that's why I've written this book.

I don't know what your Goliath is, or what your *"Stand-Off"* looks like. Your fight may be financial, physical, or emotional; it may be your marriage, your career, or your kids; it may come from a painful past, a present failure or fear of the future. *WHATEVER* your case may be – this story is for you!

The story of David and Goliath has transcended the ages as a metaphor for the "underdog." Read it carefully, because I believe it's a gift from God for anyone facing troubles bigger then themselves. You won't find a book anywhere that has *"your name"* in it, describing exactly the torments you're facing. Instead, God has given you this *"seemingly"* simple story filled with secrets to transport you from the edge of despair to a place of power and confidence.

While the skeptics, motivated by their own egos, entertain themselves debating "jots and tittles" straining at tiny details, or snicker making *"Mother Goose"* comparisons; you have the opportunity to explore the magic of this magnificent story that has been relevant to people in every culture and walk of life for over 3000 years. The story is recorded in the 17th chapter of 1 Samuel, where David squares off with Goliath in a fight to the death – but the real miracle is found in the mysterious details that will change your life today.

At some point, you will face a *"stand-off;"* a time when life grinds to a halt and there's no way out. You can't go back ...and the giant says that you can't go on - that the only future for you is to become a slave to your circumstances. However, you must resist the temptation to *"blame God"* or recite the familiar complaints on your *"why me"* list.

Remember God's will for your life.

He wants YOU to become more than a conqueror!

Romans 8:37 (NIV)
[37] No, in all these things we are more than conquerors through him who loved us.

But... just reading the above verse, or even shouting it from your comfortable church pew won't make you a conqueror because – *only battles do that!*

So right now, take a fresh survey of your life and the battlefield. Then ask God to open your heart to His love and wisdom to allow you to see the comparisons between your current struggle and the warfare David waged with Goliath. Remember that this epic battle wasn't recorded just to give us a cute story for Sunday school; it's a combat field manual to teach YOU how to be a warrior and overcome the giant size problems in your life!

So now let's look at the story again, and remember

God gave it to YOU because <u>He loves YOU</u>!
David defeated his giant …and so can YOU!

Israel was in a standoff with the Philistines in the Judean foothills known as the **Shfela.** This was a series of valleys and ridges that run east and west. One of those valleys was the valley of Elah; an extremely important corridor from the coastal towns that lead up through the center of the land to the cities of Bethlehem, Hebron and Jerusalem. It was here that Israel's greatest enemy, attempted to push through this valley towards the very heart of the kingdom of Judah. The Philistines wanted to occupy the highlands and split the kingdom in two!

That's exactly what the Enemy does…

he aims at YOUR heart!

He targets the heart of your home, your marriage, your career, and your happiness because he wants to tear your life into pieces.

John 10:10 (KJV)

10 The thief cometh not, but for to steal, and to kill, and to destroy: I am come that they might have life, and that they might have it more abundantly.

When they were discovered King Saul immediately dispatched his armies to block them, facing off with the Philistines **between** Shochoh and Azekah – *"that belonged to Judah."* 1Samuel 17:1.

I think it is significant and interesting that the name *"Shochoh"* means *"**defense**",* and *"Azekah"* means ***"strength of walls."*** Symbolically, this is a perfect illustration of the tactics of the enemy. Whether it's

Israel facing the Philistines, my mother squared off with me in her bedroom; or the enemy you're facing in your life right now. The plan of the enemy is to drive like a dagger toward the very heart of your existence and "pitched their camp" __*between*__ your "defenses," and your "strengths."

My mother loved me completely and I loved her, but the giant in me had wounded the very heart of her. I still remember, with <u>great regret</u>, the desperation and sadness I brought into her life. Through my selfish ways I broke down her defenses and robbed her of her joy and strength. She was paralyzed in a stalemate of confusion wondering what to do with a child that had turned into a rebellious teenage monster. Just like the standoff between Israel and the Philistines, we both had taken our positions on opposite sides of the corridor that led to the heart of our happiness.

What was she supposed to do? What are you supposed to do when you're faced with a battle that's bigger then you can win? She decided that if she couldn't win the battle with me head-on, at least she wouldn't do anything to make it worse. She chose to find some high-ground, to hold on to what little power she had left; and that is exactly what Israel did too.

The Philistines took positions in the mountains located on the south side of the valley, while the Israelites pitched their camps in the mountains on the north side.

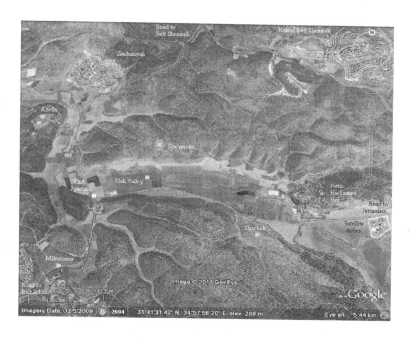

The aerial view shows the valley of Elah and includes the ancient sites of Azeka, and Shochoh. The Elah stream loops around the edge of the hill on its way north-west.

It's a common strategy to seize the high ground. Everyone knows that in combat the army that holds the high ground has the advantage. Certainly both

Israel and the Philistines knew it and they weren't about to leave their *"high ground"* mountain positions.

The city of Azekah, is seen here on top of a hill in the center of the far background. This picture shows the north-west side of the valley.

To break the deadlock, the Philistines used an ancient tradition known as "single combat" to avoid mass casualties. They sent Goliath to challenge Israel to end the standoff with a single fight between two champions - one from each side. Goliath, was a 13 ft., 4 in., Philistine Giant heavily armed with a 10lb sword, a 10lb. helmet of brass and a coat of mail that weighed 194 lbs. He had coverings of brass on his legs, a plate of brass between his shoulders, a spear the size of a "weaver's beam," with a spearhead that weighed over 23lbs. And… he was preceded by a shield bearer that *"went before him,"* carrying a 30lb shield.

And so it began…
EVERY DAY …TWICE A DAY …for FORTY DAYS!
Goliath taunted King Saul and Israel.

1 Samuel 17: 8-10 & 16
"And he stood and called out to the armies of Israel and said unto them: Why are you come out to set your battle in array? Am I not a Philistine and you are the servants to Saul? **Choose a man** and <u>let him come down to me</u>. If he is able to fight with me and kill me, then we will be your servants: but if I prevail against him and kill him, then you will be our servants, and serve us. And the Philistine said, I defy the armies of Israel this day; **give me a man** that <u>we may fight together</u>".

In verse 16
"**Each morning and evening <u>for 40 days</u>**, the Philistine came forward and made his challenge."

What is your strategy when you're in the fight of your life, or for someone that you love?

You could be facing rebellion like my mother faced with me; or maybe addiction, depression, sickness, failure or one of a thousand other giants that march their way into the heart of your life. How can you possibly overcome?

It is perfectly natural and responsible to look for anything on earth that can give you an advantage. My mother sought everyone she thought may help. She would have tried anything to gain the upper hand and save her son. She called on the courts, counselors, churches, friends, family, pastors, and the police. Some people reach out to doctors, drugs, medicines and treatments of every kind imaginable; and sometimes those choices end with disastrous results.

But what else can you do... when nothing helps?

That verse in the story stands out, painting a life picture like a haunting theme of hopeless despair.

> **1 Samuel 17:16** King James Version (KJV)
> [16] And ***the Philistine drew near morning and evening***, and presented himself forty days.

Before breakfast ...you could see him coming! Every morning he was there to the ruin the day and take away any thoughts of victory. As he paraded back and forth screaming his vile threats the gleaming sunlight reflected off the massive shield of brass.

The eerie sound of that enormous frightening sword clanging on his side intimidated any one that was watching. He poisoned the air with insults and accusations; ridiculing and mocking the strength of Israel goading them to a fight. The continuous sound of his heckling and the jangling noise of his armor penetrated the hearts of Israel's mighty men, slowly hemorrhaging their hope and courage.

Every night when the men laid down to sleep, anxious anticipation robbed their eyes of rest. The peaceful silence of the evening was shattered by the ranting mad man, terrorizing them again and again. Their once triumphant dreams are consumed with terror; wondering if they would suffer a horrifying death or dismemberment. Surely for some, it wasn't long before the thought of living life as a slave was a welcomed alternative to the torture they were destined to endure.

So it continued...
EVERY DAY ...TWICE A DAY ...for FORTY DAYS!

Does this sound familiar?

I have spoken to many broken hearted parents of rebellious children. I've listened to the anguish of spouses and siblings of alcohol and drug addicted loved ones. I have seen the misery of those battling anxiety and depression and host of other giant size problems. There is one sad and glaring characteristic they all endure; it's the physical and mental exhaustion caused by the relentless attacks and unceasing erosion of their hope and happiness. The enemy is relentless! Evil is like the darkness ...just waiting to invade the absence of light.

EVERY DAY ...TWICE A DAY
...it NEVER SEEMS to STOP!

I know she loved me, but I'm sure, like when the Israelites saw Goliath ...my mother hated to see me coming. It was always the same ...eventually I would be parading back and forth hurling my crushing insults and demands. I also wonder how many children of alcoholics run for cover when they see the parent they love turn into a raging fool screaming razor-sharp hateful words.

The lives of all those facing the assaults of these heavily armored giants mirror one another. There's little difference between their lives and those of the once mighty men of Saul's army. The anger, insults, accusations, excuses, the persistent threats, and the endless disappointments destroy all hope for real happiness. So many families, like Saul's once triumphant army, look okay from the outside but have been destroyed within under the weight of overwhelming fear. Humiliated and exhausted they mentally surrender; willing to live their lives as a slave to their circumstances. They pray for miracle every night – but the giant keeps on coming!

EVERY DAY ...TWICE A DAY ...HE NEVER STOPS!

When the miracle doesn't come, fear and desperation prevails, and they scream blaming God – wailing "Why me?"

The one thing they don't consider...
...that
THEY could be the MIRACLE!

The great King Saul, his mighty warriors, and the entire army of Israel was being controlled by ONE man – Goliath. That's what giants do! They control and intimidate by their sheer size and power; the very sight of them strikes fear into everyone's heart. That's what your giants want to do to you. Like magicians, they depend on your distraction. They want you to focus with their size and "perceived strength;" while they intimidate you with rage, and destroy your faith with lies. They intend to enslave your life with anxiety and fear - after all, what experience do you have fighting giants?

I clearly remember the day my older cousin told me how to *"always get my way"* with my mother. He charged me to confront her head-on. He pointed out that she was a women, a single mother, and too weak to overpower me; and she wouldn't dare call the police on her own son – she loved me too much!

He taught me exactly what to say to make her back down and give in to my demands. She would have no choice. He told me to wait for just the right moment, raise my voice and declare:

> *"I'm on LSD right now!*
> *What are you going to do about it?"*
> (sound familiar?)

My cousin and I (Goliath), and your giant too, are all counting of one thing; that you will collapse in fear – never realize that... ***God can make YOU the miracle!***

We ALWAYS tend to look at the immediate circumstances and never consider the big picture. Goliath, like so many with a fleshly worldview, thought that the fight was just about the present battle. That it's all about him and his foe; their goals and conquest. Every decision Goliath and the Philistines considered was based upon their own strengths. They wanted to beat Israel down, to wear them out, to humiliate them and make them slaves. Goliath reminded them of that fact...

EVERY DAY ...TWICE A DAY ...for FORTY DAYS!

Israel never dreamed that through this "stand-off" God would raise up a man, and a miracle; and Israel had no idea that this confrontation would set the stage for the greatest Kingdom they would ever see!

"Little" David was still in the fields tending the sheep and didn't realize that he was about to change the world; and my mother never imagined that one day I would write this book for you...

...and you may not know right now, but

God doesn't want to give you a miracle, He wants to MAKE YOU ONE!

Terry W. Bomar

Chapter 2

Marching off to Nowhere!

A defiant Giant, screaming at the top of his lungs is the first thing they hear every morning and the last thing they hear every night; and what is the great army of Israel doing - they're marching.

The opposing armies were stretched out along each side of the valley. There were a few skirmishes from time to time, but nothing was really happening. Nothing was happening except for Goliath's daily tirade and Israel's "good intentions" to do something about it; in the mean time they marched.

In verse 8, Goliath mocked them, defying them to *"send a man"* that was willing to take him on. He laughed at the "army" and the "mighty King Saul."

> **8** And he stood and cried unto the armies of Israel, and said unto them, Why are ye come out to set your battle in array? am not I a Philistine, and ye servants to Saul? choose you a man for you, and let him come down to me.

What was the goal of Goliath and the Philistines? Verse 9 says: it was to "make them slaves."

> **9** If he be able to fight with me, and to kill me, then will we be your servants: but if I prevail against him and kill him, then shall ye be our servants and *serve us.*

What was the reaction of Saul and Israel? They were "intimidated" and "very afraid".

> **10** And the Philistine said, I defy the armies of Israel this day; give me a man, that we may fight together.
> **11** When Saul and all Israel heard those words of the Philistine, they were dismayed and *greatly afraid.*

What was Israel "actually" doing to win the war with the Philistines?

- In verse 8, they were "setting" the battle in array.
- In verse 20, they were "going forth" to the fight and "shouted" for the battle.
- In verse 21, they had "set" the battle in array (...again).
- But in verse 24, when they "saw" him, <u>they ran from him</u>, and <u>they were afraid of him</u>!

Their good intentions and their actions didn't match their true feelings. What they were doing outwardly was the opposite of how they felt inwardly. Several times it indicates that they "set" for battle ...but there was NO battle!

> *They were "going forth to fight"*
> *....but there was NO fight!*

> *They "shouted for the battle"*
> *...but it was just noise without warfare!*

They were going through the motions they'd done a thousand times before, but when it came time to fight ...they were content to march.

I can see them as they busied themselves polishing their armor and preparing their uniforms. No doubt they were meticulous in their dress, everything had to look perfect. Their helmets, breastplates and shields must have looked like mirrors in the desert sun. I'm sure the soldiers spent hours practicing battle techniques and honed their swords to a razor-sharp edge.

When everything was ready, when everything was perfect, it was time to march; and boy they had it down. They marched in perfect formation, no one missed a step. When I picture them parading past King Saul for inspection I can almost hear the cadence of the war chants they shouted in perfect unison. Their marching demonstration would raise the hair on the back of your neck. There was nothing like it! When one company paraded by, all the other companies watched with awe as they prepared for their turn to march. Each commander drilled his men over and over again because they all wanted to catch the eye of King Saul. They wanted everyone to know that they looked the best, sounded the best ...and marched the best.

When all the companies came together it was a sight to behold. The spectacle of this magnificent army walking in perfect precision left you breathless. But the sound... the sound of their thunderous voices was overwhelming. Everyone that saw them was consumed with emotion - they were the greatest army on earth!

Until...

Until they "saw" him.
He was just one man, but the mere sight of this one man changed everything ...but how?

What changed everything was not the height of Goliath, or his armor, or even his constant ranting; what changed everything were the assumptions in the heart of Saul's army. When they "saw" him, his size alone spawned all kinds of ideas in their heart.

As with many people, I'm sure those assumptions were also fueled by gossip and innuendo coming from every "wanna-be" General in the army. They were fixated on the giant and they couldn't see anything else. Their own hearts betrayed them because they no longer believed in themselves. They didn't realize that they had emotionally surrendered before they had even drawn a sword. Instead, they did what they were good at ...they marched.

They did what made them feel good. They busied themselves with a diversion so they wouldn't have to think about that giant in the valley below. They slipped into a state of denial so they wouldn't have to confront the one screaming at them...

EVERY DAY ...TWICE A DAY ...for FORTY DAYS!

They chose the safety of the mountain tops, they did what made them feel good, they did what they were good at, they did what gave them hope

...what's wrong with that?

Nothing's wrong with that ...if this is just a fairy tale. But life isn't a fairy tale and what they were facing was real. What my mother faced was real. What you're facing today is real. If they were going to hold on to their country, their heritage and their families – they were going to have to fight! They couldn't stay in the mountains forever and neither can you.

Doing what made them feel good temporarily served only to slowly destroy them internally. Doing what they were good at only served to remind them of "who" they really should be and what they were supposed to be doing. Doing what gave them hope?

False hope ...is no hope at all!

It's easy to surrender your life to the comforts of denial like Israel was doing. It's much easier to ignore the giants in your life, then it is to fight them - especially if they're screaming at you every day!

Who could blame you for wanting to deny that your child, your spouse, or you yourself are addicted to drugs or alcohol? No one wants to take on that giant? No one!

There are multitudes of giants to face in this life. You may be facing your greatest adversary or trial right now, at this very moment. Every day you may be tempted to just bury your head in the sand and accept your life as it is ...after all ...like some people say: "everything happens for a reason!" But ...that "saying" is a lie; and It will rob you of your destiny! Your destiny will not be determined by what "happens," but by your obedience (or disobedience) to God's will.

If you ignore the giant, you'll slowly surrender your life piece by piece until all that's important to you is gone. You cannot stay in the mountain tops just to avoid the battle you know you have to fight in the valley. You can't soothe real life problems with syrupy platitudes and "bumper-sticker" theology. Life is real... and your giant is real.

He is NOT going away...
until someone defeats him in a real battle!

Instead of fighting the "real" battle
we just.... What?

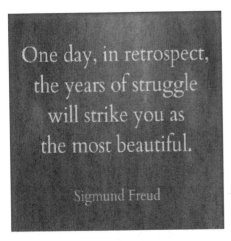

One day, in retrospect, the years of struggle will strike you as the most beautiful.

Sigmund Freud

What diversion are you taking?

Are you just pretending to address the siege?

Maybe you're satisfied to fight a thousand little skirmishes and ignore the real problem that's been screaming at you every day. Or maybe... you've already thrown away your sword and surrendered your life emotionally ...to just do what makes you feel good?

Are you willing to "pretend" happiness with a "pretend" army and just march? What kind of marching are you doing? At some point we ALL do it. We mindlessly march along as parents, spouses, employers, companies, and even churches ...especially churches. Wow! We church folk may not like dancing but we sure love to march.

We the church, are described as the "light of the world" capable of driving out the darkness – anywhere we shine. We've been called the "salt" of the earth; not just by "anyone" – Jesus called us that! Although common today, throughout history salt has been one of the most valuable substances in the world. But far too often the church has lost its "saltiness" and become caught-up in the "marching." Some churches focus on getting the "dress" just right, some on the "shouting," others want to get the "form" in its "proper order," while others just sit around polishing their armor and sharpening their swords.

We "march in" every Sunday, singing and shouting, parading our army before the Lord ...but who is fighting the giant? Inspired by thrilling sermons from our commanders and full of good intentions we march out again ..."going forth" to fight!

Until...

Until Monday morning when we "see" the giant that looks bigger than ourselves. Until we hear the hurtful words of a rebellious child or spouse. Until... until... until... we see that ole familiar sin or giant that has been mocking us for days, weeks or years.

Until... Sunday rolls around ...time to march again!

Sometimes we can become so committed to our church, our company, our commanders and our marching; that we forget what we're marching for. If our uniforms are spotless, our songs are inspiring, and our marching is perfect ...but giants are filling our homes and land ...we missed the point.

When marching becomes more important than slaying giants we're in trouble!

If we become so satisfied with the sounds of our own songs and sermons that we can ignore the taunting giant or hear the cries of his victims every night on the evening news; then we 've forgotten our purpose.

You know we're in denial if we spend more time polishing our armor than we spend protecting people. And when we ignore the real problems we start fighting the wrong people. We fight more with each other then we do with giants. We should never be better at marching than we are at making a difference.

Most people agree that the world is in deep trouble; and usually everyone shakes their fists at the darkness blaming some form of evil. The problem with that thought is that evil doesn't get "more" evil; just like darkness doesn't get "more" dark.

Darkness doesn't get darker...
the "light" just gets dimmer.

EVERY DAY... SEVERAL TIMES A DAY...

We hear the Goliaths of evil spreading their threats on the 24 hour news channels. Every day they challenge us to send them "A MAN or A WOMAN" who would dare to defeat them and change the world for good.

YOU!
...could be
THAT PERSON!

You may have been in a standoff for a long time, facing the same ole giant – but it doesn't have to stay that way. You can be the person that makes all the difference. You can change yourself, your family, your child, your spouse, your church, and your community. It does NOT matter what... or who your giant may be... YOU can beat them! Remember... ALL giants look the same; they're always bigger, louder, and well-armed. They always accuse, intimidate, threaten and mock you. The greatest military in the world became "afraid" when they SAW him. You can't fix your "focus" on the your giant ...but on your victory!

You can defeat your giant if...

- You don't get distracted.
- You don't get diverted
- You don't get satisfied
- You don't get afraid...

You cannot allow yourself to become "distracted" by the size of your problem. Or "distracted" by the ferocity of his threats. Your focus should be on the God who loves you, who called you and who promised you that *HE* would be with you.

Hebrews 13:6 (NIV)
[6] So we say with confidence,
"The Lord is my helper; I will not be afraid.
What can mere mortals do to me?"

Psalm 28:7 (NIV)
[7] The Lord is my strength and my shield; my heart trusts in him, and he helps me. My heart leaps for joy, and with my song I praise him.

2 Corinthians 10:3-5 (NIV)
[3] For though we live in the world, we do not wage war as the world does. [4] The weapons we fight with are not the weapons of the world. On the contrary, they have divine power to demolish strongholds. [5] We demolish arguments and every pretension that sets itself up against the knowledge of God, and we take captive every thought to make it obedient to Christ.

You cannot get "diverted" by the little skirmishes or become occupied with false hopes. I can still remember all the confusion my actions caused my mother in so many ways. The attacks and problems may come at you from a dozen directions. Trying to fight them all will leave you overwhelmed, confused and depressed. The "simple answers," from well-intentioned friends may leave you feeling empty - because clichés won't do; and they keep you diverted with false hopes that fail. To beat a giant, you MUST first acknowledge that it's indeed a giant ...and you're expecting God's help!.

You cannot allow yourself to be "diverted" by just "words" or a "positive confession." You have to IDENTIFY your giant, hear from God and follow His guidance. Moses faced the King of Egypt. He obeyed God... and we all know how that turned out!

Moses overcame because
he "SAW" God, instead of his enemy.

Hebrews 11:27 New International Version (NIV)
[27] By faith he left Egypt, not fearing the king's anger; he persevered ***because he saw him who is invisible.***

You cannot become satisfied with just marching, polishing, primping, or pretending everything is okay. You can't be satisfied with "praying about it"

***...it's NOT prayers you need,
it's ANSWERS to PRAYERS that you need!***

In the New Testament, people were constantly trying to make others be satisfied with less than what God had for them. The people crowded out one woman with an "issue of blood." But she would NOT be satisfied with just seeing Jesus ...she was determined to TOUCH JESUS!

Some tried to stop a blind Bartimaeus from crying out to Jesus for his healing. But he would NOT be satisfied with just hearing Jesus ...he wanted to SEE JESUS!

Neither were satisfied "just marching" to someone else's orders; and the answer from Jesus to both of them was the same:

Luke 8:48 King James Version (KJV)
[48] And he said unto her, Daughter, be of good comfort: <u>**thy faith**</u> **hath made thee whole**; go in peace.

Mark 10:52 King James Version (KJV)
[52] And Jesus said unto him, Go thy way; <u>**thy faith**</u> **hath made thee whole**. And immediately he received his sight, and followed Jesus in the way.

You cannot be afraid. Fear is the greatest weapon of your enemy. When they "saw" the giant, they ran from him BECAUSE they were so AFRAID. Fear is the natural response to danger and uncertainty. Warfare is full of danger and fear, whether it's a battle of bombs and bullets or sharp swords of wounding words.

I know my mother was afraid "for me," and she was afraid "of me." Fear is always present and there WILL be times when you are afraid; but you can overcome it with faith. The first person you have to convince that *"you're not afraid"* - is YOU!

Psalm 56:2-4 New International Version (NIV)
² My adversaries pursue me all day long;
   in their pride many are attacking me.
³ **When** I am afraid, I put my trust in you.
⁴   In God, whose word I praise—
in God I trust and am not afraid.
   What can mere mortals do to me?

For a long time my mom "marched" to church and marched back home again. She did it because she didn't know what else to do with me. She was afraid of me, or what might happen if she did the wrong thing. She tried to appease me, entertain me, preach to me and plead with me; but nothing worked.

Until….

Until she stopped marching. One night she went to church and she'd had enough. This time, she did something about it. She didn't "pray about me," she touched God! When she came home that night she knew who she was, she knew that I was her son and she wasn't about to let the devil have my life …and she brought her faith and courage with her.

I was laying on the bed in my bedroom when she kicked open my door …with a message from God that changed my life forever.
         THE "MARCHING" WAS OVER!

Chapter 3

The Seeds of Greatness

Someone once said, *"the mighty Oak tree is simply the result of a little nut that held its ground."* It may be funny, but it's true. Miracles are not magic tricks and God isn't a magician. Your life isn't a "show" and God doesn't "perform" to impress you or prove Himself to you. Miracles are wondrous gifts from God that are made possible in two ways; either by the divine intervention of God, or the result of obedience and application of God's Word that brings about "God's will" in a supernatural way. Just like seeds, miracles often begin in the damp and darkest places of our lives. Seeds themselves aren't magic either, but the process that springs them to life is a miracle. Several conditions converge to set the stage for the miracle of life that we take for granted every day.

Right now, you may be facing the darkest moments in your life. You may feel cut-off,

THE TINY SEED KNEW THAT IN ORDER TO GROW IT NEEDED to be dropped in dirt, COVERED IN DARKNESS, AND STRUGGLE TO reach the light.

DAYSTAR

all alone and out of touch from everyone else around you. The circumstances may feel cold and damp, dark and lonely but they're also the perfect conditions for a miracle!

Far from the sound of battle sat a young boy named David. He dreamed of being a warrior, a champion for God and his country. But instead of defending his family and friends, he was babysitting a few sheep. There were no weapons of warfare, no marching mighty men, no battle cries or cheering crowds. The only sounds he heard were coming from a band of boring animals. He yearned for a life of purpose, but no doubt felt trapped in a meaningless existence of mundane tasks. As the youngest, with seven older brothers, he must have felt overlooked and unappreciated quite often. One clear example of this was when his father was asked of Samuel to present his sons to him, Jesse didn't even call David from the field until "after" Samuel specifically asked if he had any other sons. Did Jesse "forget" David, or did he not think David was important enough to be considered?

David's father Jesse often referred to his brother's strong physical attributes and natural abilities for battle, but David was described as "the youngest," "ruddy," thin, reddish or red haired (possibly blonde), and nice looking. Today, those attributes are great ...if your desire is to be magazine model for Calvin Klein, but it certainly didn't look great on a resume if you wanted to be a warrior in Israel. When you hear these depictions and read many of the Psalms, you realize that he may have struggled with the inner turmoil of self-doubt and low self-esteem. David dreamed of being a "mighty man" but no one else (not even in his own family) could see him as he saw himself.

The greater the passion, the greater the conflict when it's denied. When deep personal desires go unfulfilled the person can feel desperate and face the greatest tests of their life. Some will give-up and just shrink away into a life of depression, satisfied to live life as a victim. Some will exalt themselves in pride and arrogance to do anything necessary to achieve their selfish goals - fooling themselves that *"the ends justify the means."* Those that choose to live their life with the *"I'm gonna get mine"* attitude and will even forsake their principles and their faith in God. But there are those that will stay true to their values and discover their own seeds of greatness ...David was one of these. During the storms of life when everything seems lost and dark they learn to reach up to God and reach down into themselves.

That's the essence of the verses in James 1, that seem perplexing (at first) when it says to *count it all joy* when various trials (storms) come upon you.

James 1:2-4

2 Consider it pure joy, my brothers and sisters, [a]whenever you face trials of many kinds, 3 because you know that the testing of your faith produces perseverance. 4 Let perseverance finish its work so that you may be mature and complete, not lacking anything.

David surely must have felt that his life was wasting away in the distant fields watching a handful of sheep while others were waging war in the name of the Lord. I wonder how many times he felt *"Why ME?"* I'm also sure that he must have questioned God and complained more than once how *"life just doesn't seem fair."* All those feelings and thoughts are normal, and every great man or woman of faith has had them – you're not alone.

The question you ask is WHY did it say to consider it ***"pure joy"*** when you face various hardships and distress? Obviously God looks at our trials VERY different than we do. It's obvious that the adversities, the hot barren desert, the lonely wilderness, ...ALL of them can have a purpose in our future – IF WE allow them too.

You may not know it now, but those are the places where the seeds of greatness are determined. It's in those places like the lonely fields where David watched his sheep that you will decide _what_ to spend your life on; and you'll choose what's important and what isn't ...because

It's the storms that separate average men from the mighty ones.

But, sometimes it isn't the raging storm that's the toughest to weather, it's the slow monotonous grind when it seems like nothing good is happening and you're all alone. You may feel that you aren't important, that even God has forgotten you. That's when you have decisions to make, and those decisions – your decisions – will shape the rest of your life forever.

This is *YOUR LIFE*, either *YOU SHAPE IT* or someone else will...

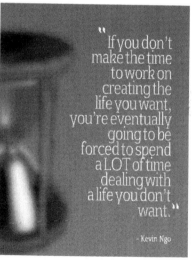

"If you don't make the time to work on creating the life you want, you're eventually going to be forced to spend a LOT of time dealing with a life you don't want."

- Kevin Ngo

He may have felt overlooked, but David decided that his integrity was more important than his ambition. When he became bored with the mundane task of babysitting sheep he made the decision that his ethics were more important than his ego. And when his pride and passion rose up with overwhelming impatience he chose to be faithful in the small things and trust God with his future.

1 Peter 5:6-7
[6] Humble yourselves, therefore, under God's mighty hand, that he may lift you up in due time. [7] Cast all your anxiety on him because he cares for you.

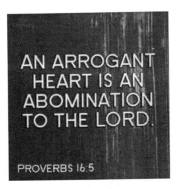

AN ARROGANT HEART IS AN ABOMINATION TO THE LORD.

PROVERBS 16:5

He may not have realized it at the time, but with each decision, and with each choice he was shaping his priorities, building his character and cultivating his faith in the God he served.

He overcame every question and every doubt by turning to God – not away from him. Every confusion caused him to dig deeper, try harder, seek God more and grow stronger every day. The seeds of greatness were being planted.

Rather than complaining or blaming God...

*HE CHOSE TO BELIEVE **GOD**...*
*HE CHOSE TO TRUST **GOD**...*
*AND HE CHOSE TO WAIT ON **GOD**.*

42

David's decisions to believe, trust and wait on God ultimately shaped his daily choices and actions. By surrendering his hopes and dreams and future into God's hand he was free to focus on his faithfulness to God; and being prepared for whatever service God would ask of him. He demonstrated the truth of Ecclesiastes 9:10 and "whatever he did, he did with all his might..." David's desire became singular and personal between him and God; he desired only to please God.

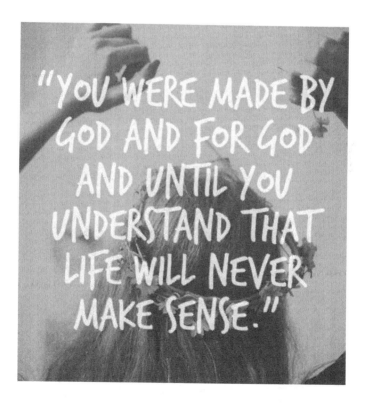

"YOU WERE MADE BY GOD AND FOR GOD AND UNTIL YOU UNDERSTAND THAT LIFE WILL NEVER MAKE SENSE."

Psalm 37:4 (NIV)
⁴ Take delight in the Lord,
   and he will give you the desires of your heart.

Being a Shepherd is a lonely, thankless job; but it
was in those lonely places that David decided what
kind of person he was going to be. He decided what
and who he was going to believe. David's choices
shaped his character, his actions and his personality.
As a result his faith was no longer in himself, but in
the God to whom he had committed his life –
regardless of the circumstances.

If he was being trusted to watch sheep, then he was
going to be the best shepherd the sheep ever had
because everything he did – he did unto the Lord.

He filled the lonely afternoons practicing with his
sling to protect his sheep from the wolves and foxes
that would threaten them. Some have said that a
skilled shepherd with a sling could hit a bird in flight
at fifty yards. Two great illustrations of David's
faithfulness, character and strength as a shepherd
was when faced enemies bigger than himself, on at
least two occasions. Once it was a lion and another
time it was a bear.

He said they came…
 "and took a lamb out of the flock." I Sam. 17:34-35

David responded both times the same way:

He went after them; he killed them; and he took the lamb out of their mouth!

And when the lion came at David ...David caught him by the beard and killed him! David's faithfulness wouldn't allow him to lose a single lamb. He risked his life to *"go after them."* David's courage wouldn't allow him to run from fear. He faced the lion, caught him, and killed him. David's character wouldn't allow him to look the other way. Dead or alive... still David risked his own life to take the lamb out of the lion's mouth!

What seeds are you planting in your life today?

Greed or Greatness

Courage or Cowardice

Faithlessness or Faithfulness

Choose your seeds carefully...

because soon you'll see them growing
in your children.

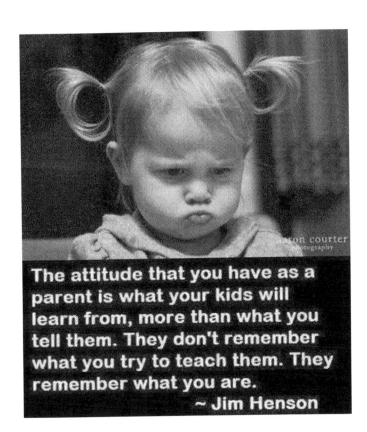

The attitude that you have as a parent is what your kids will learn from, more than what you tell them. They don't remember what you try to teach them. They remember what you are.
~ Jim Henson

Chapter 4

Who Moved My Cheese?

Many years ago Dr. Spencer Johnson created a story to help him deal with a difficult change in his life. It was a simple tale about four characters that ran through an intricate maze in search of cheese to nourish them and make them happy. Two of them were mice named *Sniff* and *Scurry*; and the other two were *"little people"* as small as mice, (beings much like us), named *Hem* and *Haw*.

The *story* changed Dr. Johnson's life and the lives of millions more. In fact, twenty years after he created the story, he published it as a book named *"Who Moved My Cheese?"* It became a #1 Best Seller with over 1 million hard copies printed in the first 16 months. In the first five years it sold over 21 million copies. Obviously, his fairy tale about four little creatures searching for their own brand of cheese struck a common nerve - that all of us are in a frantic search for something to make us happy.

Sometimes, like in the early life of David, we may be *"dying for a change;"* we feel unappreciated, overlooked and trapped in our circumstances. At other times change itself is the enemy; like an unexpected storm that blows in to destroy our happy lives. But...

WHAT DOES CHEESE HAVE TO DO WITH IT?

First, let's look at it from Dr. Johnson's perspective in his tale comparing the rodents and *"the little people."* He masterfully weaves together the different tastes and tactics of mice and men in a wonderful example of how our own minds and complexities keep us from the very happiness that we seek.

The lowly mice, *"Sniff and Scurry,"* scamper their way through the complex maze by trial and error to find cheese. They never become complacent or conflicted, they simply enjoy the cheese they find and move-on to find more when the cheese is gone. While at the same time, the intellectual "little people" become first indulgent and later feeling entitled to the cheese "they found," they become trapped by their disappointments when the cheese runs out. They become prisoners to their own assumptions of entitlement, fear and depression; wailing in despair that life just isn't fair. They accuse each other, soon becoming consumed with anger and denial they just *"Hem and Haw,"* waiting for "someone" to confess...

"Who Moved My Cheese?"

I'll let Dr. Johnson tell the rest of the story when you read his book; but I will say that it's an excellent example of the truth and power of motivational thinking. At times, we all become over-confident in our own abilities. We get complacent and indulgent expecting everything to always stay the same; and when change happens - we're shocked and angry!

Humility isn't a "suggestion" from God, it's a gift of divine protection for you. Pride and ego grows easily into arrogance and entitlement; all of which increases the pain when change comes – and it will. If you aren't careful, your disappointments will turn into a life of anger and resentment. Then you'll start blaming God and everyone else in sight for "moving your cheese!"

Some think that as a Christian, you can't learn from such "worldly" wisdom; but actually the very opposite is true. In fact, the principles of most motivational speeches can be traced back to the book of Proverbs and others. Jesus even used an example of the "unjust" manager to demonstrate it:

> **Luke 16:8** (NIV)
> [8] "The master commended the dishonest manager because he had acted shrewdly. For the people of this world are more shrewd in dealing with their own kind than are the people of the light.

Now, let's take a look at "your cheese" from God's point of view. You were created in His image. You were designed to "go forth," to "replenish" and "subdue" the earth. Your desires to accomplish, create, build and grow were all given to you by your Creator; and God is pleased by the prosperity of His people. God loves cheese!

Psalm 35:27b (KJV)
"...Let the Lord be magnified, which hath pleasure in the prosperity of his servant.

The Word of God makes several promises concerning the desires and satisfactions of your heart when you put Him first.

Here's a few of *"YOUR CHEESE"* related promises:

Psalm 37:4 (NIV) [4] Take delight in the Lord,
and he will give you the desires of your heart.

Matthew 6:33 (NIV) [33] But seek first his
kingdom and his righteousness, and all these
things will be given to you as well.

Proverbs 3:6 (NIV) [6] in all your ways submit to
him, and he will make your paths straight.

1 Corinthians 2:9 (KJV) [9] But as it is written, Eye
hath not seen, nor ear heard, neither have
entered into the heart of man, the things which
God hath prepared for them that love him.

Ephesians 3:20 (KJV) [20] Now unto him that is
able to do exceeding abundantly above all that
we ask or think, according to the power that
worketh in us,

Luke 6:38 (NIV) [38] Give, and it will be given to
you. A good measure, pressed down, shaken
together and running over, will be poured into
your lap. For with the measure you use, it will
be measured to you."

The difference between the "daily cheese" that the average person is seeking and the cheese that God has prepared for them is defined by one word...

PURPOSE

I'm sure that young David loved *"cheese"* just as much as the next guy. He dreamed of being successful, powerful and rich just like any young man might do at his age. David had the classic "A-type" personality and I'm sure his burning ambitions created a great internal conflict that he wrestled with daily. But, I'm also sure that in those times of devotion when he poured out his heart to God; that he gained a sense of confidence that God had a plan and purpose for his life.

> **Psalm 138:8** English Standard Version (ESV)
> [8] The Lord will fulfill his purpose for me;
>   your steadfast love, O Lord, endures forever.
>   Do not forsake the work of your hands.

David's determination to find and follow God's will controlled his ambition. However, I'm sure that many times he was pushed to the brink by the constant "baaas" of the sheep – while his brothers were basking in glories of War. I'm sure that he must have been tempted to think that he was wasting his life and that his chance would never come ...but one day it did come.

David's **"BIG BREAK..."**
the one that he had been waiting for all his life...
...CAME ON A CHEESE PLATTER!

You may be very close to your "big break" right now
and still miss it ...if your focus is on the wrong
things. To fully understand, try to put yourself in
David's shoes. You're the youngest, and the
smallest, of eight boys in the family. You have a
proud family heritage in Israel. In your heart burns
the passion of a warrior but you've been stuck for
years tending sheep; and even your father doesn't
see your potential because he's all caught up in the
physical attributes of your big brothers.

Now, the alarm has sounded that the Philistines
have set themselves in position and they're
threatening to take over the country. The armies of
Israel are preparing for battle: and where is David?
...still saddled with the sheep. Then to *add insult to
injury* he gets word that he can accompany his
father and brothers *to see them off to the war*.

So they make the journey to front lines where David
sees the Officers and thousands of soldiers in
preparation for war. The sound of horses and
marching men fill the air and perhaps he even gets a
glimpse of King Saul; but then it's time to leave. He
leaves his brothers to fight for the glory of Israel
while he plods his way back to the forgotten field of

sheep. One more time, David has to choose to trust God with his dreams of greatness. The next few nights must have been pure agony as David tried to sleep as he tossed and turned dreaming about the war. Little did he know that the next morning a simple servant's task would change his life forever.

Once again word came from his father, asking David to carry a load of bread and *cheese* to his brothers and the other men in the camp. It wasn't long before the new *"boy waiter"* was loaded down not with battle swords but with bread; not with polished shields of armor but with smelly sacks of cheese. It must have been humiliating for a boy who dreamed of leading an army, to walk into the camp leading only a donkey. No one even considered that David was good enough to fight. Their words burned ...cutting through his heart like a knife:

"Just give us our food and go home boy!
Go back to those sheep ...where you belong."

BUT NOT THIS TIME!
NOT THIS DAY ...AND NOT THIS BATTLE

BECAUSE GOD...
JUST MOVED HIS CHEESE!

You may feel like you've been forgotten; that your turn is never going to come around. You may think that no one cares or understands what you're going through. You might believe that there's no way out of the mess you're in and you're ready to give up.

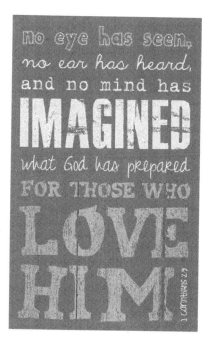

But, if you love God and you're faithful to Him read this story again and remember...

***God can find you in an empty field
...or on the moon!***

And God doesn't have to shake heaven and earth to change your circumstances...

***God can change your life
with a plate full of cheese!***

Chapter 5

Magic Moments

Personally, I'm addicted to all the magnificent stories in the Bible. I've studied them throughout my entire life; and in every story you can pinpoint a specific point in time that I call *the Magic Moment.* It's the incredible instant that changes everything and David was about to have one.

Somebody once said:

"What you put up with, you will end up with."

My mother's magic moment (concerning me) came sometime while she was at church one night. She was at the end of her rope and wasn't going to put up with anymore. She was determined for a change. Maybe it was while she was praying for me at the altar or maybe it was during the sermon; I'll never know. What I do know is that at some point... "the words jumped off the page!" The Word of God *"came alive"* in her heart and mind. She understood it! She grabbed it! And... she believed it! She really touched God

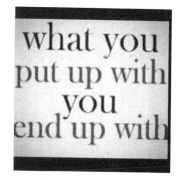

that night and was never the same. Her perception changed, her prayer changed and her actions changed. Her faith and "her actions of faith" that she brought home changed everything. She was no longer just another desperate mother begging God for answers on "how to cope with a rebellious teen." She had plugged into God's agenda, not hers. She realized that HE had a PLAN for me that was bigger than her concerns. She suddenly realized that before I was hers - I was His!

She was like David when she walked in the house, *...SHE KNEW WHO SHE WAS!* She also knew that I was her son and she wasn't about to let the devil have my life. Like David, she went *"after the enemy"* and she was determined to *"pull her little lamb right out of the lion's mouth!"*

THAT WAS A MAGIC MOMENT!

Abram had one when he left everything...
Moses had one when he forsook all of Egypt...
Elisha had one when he slipped on Elijah's mantle...

Peter had one when he stepped out of the boat...
Gideon had one when he came out of hiding...
Samson had one when he appealed to God to remember me just once more...

In every great story in the Bible you can find that single moment that changes everything.

Now, let's take look at David's Magic Moment ...and possibly yours too!

The timing was perfect. David had risen early before sunrise to travel the fifteen miles from his home to the camp of Israel. Surely he was struck with awe when he arrived just in time to see the mighty battalion marching towards the front line. (Of course, marching is all they had been doing for over a month, because no one wanted to face Goliath)

David had no idea that the great army of Israel had been stale-mated by this one man; or that now they were reduced to *"going through the motions"* pretending to ready, day after day. He was thrilled just to be close to the action and desperately wanted to be a part of it. He was so anxious that he left the wagon with the keeper and ran to find his brothers. It's almost cute that when young David did find his big brothers that he saluted them ...as if he were one the soldiers too.

I can almost see them as they greeted each other, while the big brothers showed a wide-eyed David around the camp. David brought them news from home and inquired how the battle was going. No doubt, the young man beamed with pride at the sight of his older brothers and he must have had a thousand questions as his imagination ran wild.

Then it happened, the magic moment...

DAVID HEARD SOMETHING!

The others had heard it a hundred times, and they were sick of hearing it! But they weren't David, they hadn't spent any time in those lonely places with only a few sheep and God to keep them company. They hadn't spent endless days of soul searching and seeking God; and they hadn't planted any seeds of greatness either - but David had ...and they were beginning to sprout.

They had ears that were "dull of hearing." They heard - but they had no understanding. They couldn't see beyond themselves to recognize the gravity in the words they had heard every day for forty days. They never heard it... but David only needed to hear it once!

What was the magic moment? What did David hear? He heard a giant Philistine say the same thing he said every day, for forty days. He heard Goliath thunder his contempt at Israel and scream:

"...I defy the armies of Israel! Give me a man and let us fight each other."

1 Sam 17:10 (NIV)

That was the magic moment! What David heard outraged everything he believed in and insulted the God he loved. He "heard something" that he wasn't going to put up with! When is the last time you came to a crossroad your faith? My mother was pushed to her crossroad by me; for David it was a Philistine. The question is:

what's pushing you... and what do you hear?

David heard something and once he heard it, he couldn't un-hear it. Hearing is the beginning, hearing opens the mind and demands a response. The Word says that faith comes by hearing.

Romans 10:17 (KJV)
[17] So then faith cometh *by hearing*, and hearing by the word of God.

Several times as Jesus spoke to the people in parables he would end his discourse by saying:

"he that has *ears to hear*, let him hear."

David's years studying the **WORD OF GOD...**
and searching the **HEART OF GOD...**
gave him hears sensitive to the **VOICE OF GOD**!

A mother may have a child and hear them cry a thousand times; but she instantly knows the difference if her child cries from pain or distress. David's daily communing with God in prayer had grown into a relationship. So when he "heard" the offensive words of the Philistine it wasn't about religion or nationalism – it was personal.

IT WAS A TURNING POINT...

*DAVID **HEARD** SOMETHING!*
*DAVID **KNEW** SOMETHING!*
AND...
*DAVID **DID** SOMETHING!*

When he heard it ...his mind demanded a response, because David knew something; and *KNOWING* draws something from the inside out...

Luke 6:45 (NIV)
[45] A good man brings good things out of the good stored up in his heart, and an evil man brings evil things out of the evil stored up in his heart. For the mouth speaks what the heart is full of.

The words that David heard that morning pierced him through the heart, because...

HE KNEW GOD! ...HE BELIEVED GOD!
AND... HE TRUSTED GOD!

When Goliath taunted the armies of Israel, the mighty men became "*sore afraid*" and ran away from the sight of him. But David didn't run...
because he knew something!

He *"knew"* God in good times and bad; from all those days he started with prayer. He came to know God as a Shepherd while he spent years watching sheep. And he knew God as a Father that would never leave him, as he laid down to sleep in the cold and lonely desert. He believed God as he learned and studied the ancient manuscripts. And he trusted God for his provision, for his protection and for his future.

So when his "big" brothers and the military leadership questioned his motives and ability, David's response was immediate, serious and amusing:

"Who IS this uncircumcised Philistine that he should defy the armies of the living God?"

Translation: "Just WHO does he think he is?"

"Let no one lose heart on account of this Philistine; your servant will go and fight him."

Translation: "I've GOT THIS!"

When they took David in to see the great King Saul, he pressed him to *"think about this son,"* let's be *"logical"* you're *"just a kid,"* - he's a " *warrior!"*

I'm sure that didn't sit well with David, who had been running from that *" label"* all his life. David desperately wanted to be a *warrior*, but instead he had to listen to the King declare that his enemy was warrior, but he was *"just a kid."* Ouch!

But it didn't matter what they said because…
DAVID KNEW SOMETHING!

David stood strong before King Saul and quoted a couple of stories from his resume.

1 Samuel 17:34-37 The Message (MSG)
[34-37] David said, "I've been a shepherd, tending sheep for my father. Whenever a lion or bear came and took a lamb from the flock, I'd go after it, knock it down, and rescue the lamb. If it turned on me, I'd grab it by the throat, wring its neck, and kill it. Lion or bear, it made no difference—I killed it. And I'll do the same to this Philistine pig who is taunting the troops of God. The God, who delivered me from the teeth of the lion and the claws of the bear, will deliver me from this Philistine."

Saul said, "Go. And God help you!"

Let's go over that again, shall we:

DAVID KNEW SOMETHING!

DAVID KNEW…
God Delivered him once.
…God, delivered me from the teeth of the lion and the claws of the bear…

DAVID KNEW…
God could do it again.
…God, will deliver me from this Philistine."

DAVID KNEW…
That HE was God's Man for the job!
And I'll do the same to this Philistine pig who is taunting the troops of God!

The result was another…

Turning Point!
…but this time it was for King Saul.

KING SAUL SAID:
"GO. AND GOD HELP YOU!"

DAVID DID SOMETHING!

Because David "heard" the taunts of Goliath, that challenged who he was and what he believed. He had a choice to make that demanded an answer. In similar fashion my mother had had enough of my defiance, and that night at church she heard something that demanded an answer to what and "who" she really believed. In those moments of crisis we are driven inward to determine what we believe, why we believe it, and discover if we really know God at all.

When David didn't receive the response he expected and was criticized, questioned and challenged; he dug deep to recall the God he knew had never failed him. For my mom, she stood in my bedroom door and declared that she'd put me into His hands because He had never failed her, and she wasn't about to forsake Him!

Doing anything of significance is the result of passion and confidence and David did something!
> *FIRST HE CONFRONTED HIS BROTHERS,*
> *SECOND HE CONFRONTED HIS KING SAUL*
> *...AND SOON HE WOULD CONFRONT GOLIATH!*

WHAT WILL YOU DO?

Chapter Six

The Death Trap

David started the day as a delivery boy with a wagon full of bread and cheese. As he arrived in the camp he was inspired by all of the activity and excited to meet the military heroes of his dreams. It was great at first, until he took a stand for what he believed, and then all hell broke loose. It started with his own family, when his oldest brother Eliab became so angry he started mocking and ridiculing David in front of everyone, accusing him of being conniving, selfish, proud and deceitful. When young David called on the others for help, they turned on him instead, piling on to accuse him of being a trouble maker and they took him to King Saul.

Surely, the wise ole King saw this as an opportunity to correct the foolish enthusiasm of a youngster; that was until David started talking. David scoffed at the very idea that any Philistine would defy the great army of Israel, and he pleaded for an opportunity to fight for his country. Saul flatly refused and scolded him to be realistic, Goliath was a warrior and he was just a boy. But David responded with a powerful testimony of faith that stirred the heart of the King – detailing the events of God delivering him from a lion and a bear. Saul was fascinated by the young man because he saw the confidence of his faith and the fire in his eyes. David's courage was infectious and his speech inspired the faith of Saul - but the risks couldn't be any higher.

Every day Goliath had confronted Israel to propose a "single combat" fight to the death to determine the outcome. King Saul knew that if he put his faith in this boy and David were to fight Goliath and lose... then they would all become the slaves of the Philistines. This battle wasn't just about David or his enthusiasm ...this was all or nothing!

David chance finally came – when he convinced Saul to give him the chance to fight Goliath but he almost walked into a death trap. Sometimes our greatest threats don't come from our enemies but from our friends. It's easy to be convinced by the doubts and fears of those around us.

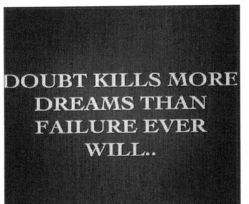

God has a purpose for YOUR life – and he wants to use YOU, not someone else.

There's a reason that you are who you are. God wasn't confused when He created you, and He doesn't make mistakes.

Psalm 139:13-15 (NIV)

[13] For you created my inmost being; you knit me together in my mother's womb.11
[14] I praise you because I am fearfully and wonderfully made; your works are wonderful, I know that full well.
[15] My frame was not hidden from you when I was made in the secret place, when I was woven together in the depths of the earth.

Before I formed you in the womb I knew you, before you were born I set you apart... Jeremiah 1:5

One of the most difficult things to do in life is to wade through the myriad of voices that seek to influence your decisions. Friends, family, co-workers, preachers, teachers, television and others all seeking to tell you how you should live.

But, if you want God's will ...you have to turn off those voices and seek God first. Shakespeare was right when he said: "to thine own self be true."

God bestowed upon you unique characteristics to achieve and fulfill the destiny for your life. When you were created, God defined your spirit with dreams and desires to inspire and motivate you; and He buried gifts and talents inside you, for you to discover and use for His glory and your success!

Saul understood David's passion for Israel; but the reality of war was heavy. Saul knew the Philistines and he saw the effect of Goliath in the hearts of his men. He watched his once mighty men cower in fear at the very sight of the man. Saul knew that Goliath was assigned to "Heavy Infantry" and wore over a hundred pounds of armor. He knew that he was skilled in close combat and intimidated everyone in his path. Every day Saul heard the titan lumber out to hurl his threatening words; and then watched his men grapple with fear. The King was acquainted with war and death and he knew that David had no chance to beat Goliath face to face.

But King Saul overlooked something. Like the others, Saul was distracted by the gigantic size of Goliath. They were all so blinded by their own perceptions and the giant's massive size they never saw his weaknesses. In their minds, the only hope was to give David as much protection as possible, and pray for mercy. So Saul dressed David with his own armor; his helmet of brass and coat of mail. Saul had the best intentions, but the wrong assumptions. Saul figured that since Goliath was "heavy infantry" that this fight would be at close quarters. Saul didn't recognize that his assumptions were allowing the enemy to define the battle - a huge tactical error!

David was never trained in warfare and certainly not in the infantry. Saul never considered the unique skills and talents of the shepherd boy. You should never allow the assumptions of others to dictate your future. You can't let their fear and perception of danger cause you to abandon your own skills. You cannot fall into the trap of trying to please others so much that you waste your own strengths by trying to wear their armor – and not your own.. Saul's armor would have been a death trap and David knew it ...he was true to himself.

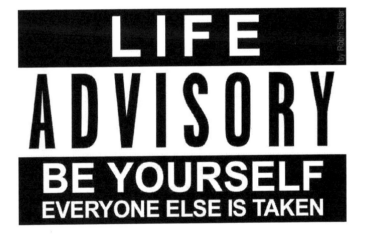

Saul was so consumed by the gravity of the battle and the size of Goliath that he never saw what he had standing right in front of him. That's the way it happens, you become so consumed with worry, and overwhelmed with problems that soon, problems are all you can see. We forget that God is with us; and we forget what we are capable of ourselves!

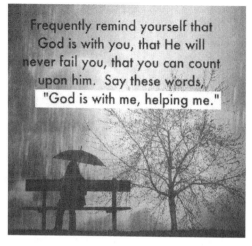

Frequently remind yourself that God is with you, that He will never fail you, that you can count upon him. Say these words, "God is with me, helping me."

David was a shepherd and he was good with a sling. Skilled slingers of the day could maim or kill a target at 200 yards and hit a bird in flight. Slingers whirled their slings at 6-8 revolutions a second and could hurl a stone with the same stopping power of a 45 caliber handgun. In many battles history records that the slingers were often the decisive factor for victory.

Other people's armor may make *"them"* feel good, but it will only weight you down. And, their ideas and tactics will keep you from being the warrior that you were meant to be. The battles that were designed for you to win will only be won with your weapons, in your hands and with your skills.

Fight your battles, with your skills
and trust your faith!
David wasn't the "underdog" ...and he knew it!

He wasn't blinded by fear. He threw off Saul's clumsy armor and chose his own weapons – a staff, a sling, and a shepherd's bag . David was a skilled slinger and "would've been" in the Artillery division. They didn't need armor because their tactics were to always be moving. David wasn't called to be Saul, he wasn't an infantryman and it would've been deadly for him to attempt it. Some people spend their lives trying to be someone else. The battle David had to fight was perfect for him and he defined the terms.

His life was about to change!
In a few minutes defeating Goliath with a sling and stone would catapult David to the throne of Israel.

Search your heart right now. Seriously think about your dreams and passion; because your passion will

"We have all been placed on this earth to discover our own path, and we will never be happy if we live someone else's idea of life!"

lead you to your purpose. Seek God's will, hear His voice. Know that God loves you and has a plan for YOU; and then even your troubles will draw you closer to Him.

1 Peter 5:6-8 (KJV)

[6] Humble yourselves therefore under the mighty hand of God, that he may exalt you in due time: [7] Casting all your care upon him; for he cares for you.

Don't be afraid to talk to God in your own way, about your life, your hopes and your troubles. Study God's Word, learn to hear God's voice and acknowledge God in all your ways:

SEEK GOD'S WILL IN ALL YOU DO, AND HE WILL SHOW YOU THE PATH TO TAKE.
PROVERBS 3:6

Romans 10:17 (KJV)
[17] So then faith cometh by hearing, and hearing by the word of God.

My mother had been to church services every week for years and attended countless seminars. She put my name on prayer lists everywhere and asked dozens of preachers to pray for me.

Nothing worked until the battle lines were drawn!

I turned our home into a combat zone, mom's life was miserable and I was on the warpath. Everybody had advice how to control a rebellious teen like me.

Their suggestions ranged from jail, to reform school and the military. Some said just ignore him, others said "tough love" was the only answer; and for some the only answer was more and more church. Thank God! Mom didn't put on everyone else's armor. She stayed true to herself and squared off with me and God face-to-face. It was personal!

It doesn't matter what your fighting - God can turn a monster into a miracle! You may be in the fight of your life trying to save your marriage, your family, your career or your health; or you may be considering some great new opportunity that could push you to the brink of greatness. Don't allow your problems to become your identity. Don't let your enemy define the battle.

Trust God and take your life back!

Your time is limited, don't waste it living someone else's life. Don't be trapped by dogma, which is living the result of other people's thinking. Don't let the noise of other's opinion drowned your own inner voice. And most important, have the courage to follow your heart and intuition, they somehow already know what you truly want to become. Everything else is secondary.

Steve Jobs

Your enemies will threaten you. Friends and family will smother you with opinions and suffocate your dreams with their fears. And don't forget the "professionals;" the "certified," the "licensed" and the "accredited" that will intimidate you, all *"...for your own good"* of course!

Know your gifts and talents. Sharpen your skills – and trust them. Don't let others hinder you with their armor, and....

Never Let the Giant Define Your Fight!

LIVE FOR GOD...

LIVE YOUR LIFE...

and wear...
YOUR ARMOR!

Terry W. Bomar

Chapter 7

Five Smooth Stones

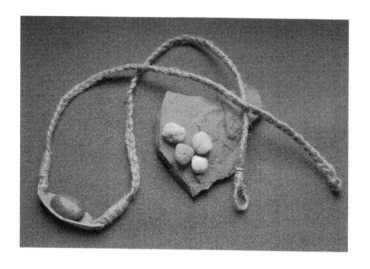

"I cannot go with these…"

With those words, David took off Saul's clumsy armor and tossed aside the massive sword. The mighty men of Israel watched with astonishment as the ruddy young boy reached for his Shepherd's staff instead. As he departed the King's tent and headed toward the valley of Elah …I can hear David muttering under his breath…

"I'm going with what got me here!"

The crowd gathered to see what the strange "glory-seeker" was going to do next. But, David distanced himself from them as he walked deeper into the valley that Goliath called his own. He wasn't looking for the giant ...not yet. He was seeking ammunition!

The spectators stood high on the hillside (safe from any conflict of course) straining to see what would become of the crazy kid. With each deliberate step David descended deeper into the gorge. He knew there had to be a brook in there somewhere and most likely it was in the lowest part of the valley; and what David needed was buried in the water.

Several years ago I made a trip to the Holy Land to see all the famous sites of the Bible. As we rumbled along the highway, the tour bus driver pointed out the basin between two hills in the distance and said, *"that's the place where David fought Goliath."* It wasn't a scheduled stop on the tour - but I wasn't about to pass this up! I have been preaching about that contest all my life. Over his objections, I finally persuaded driver to stop for "a bathroom break." When the doors opened and before he could say no, I leaped out and over the guardrail and sprinted down the hillside to the bottom – and there it was!

Just as it was 3000 years ago ...a cool little brook, hidden in the grass, meandering its way through the length of valley. Wow!

I didn't even notice that I was soaking wet reaching in the water for one stone after another. After I filled my pockets with rocks, I just sat there visualizing the two great armies on each side and the two warriors that met in that place so long ago. But suddenly... I was shocked back to the future by the blaring horn of a tour bus and its irate driver! Every time I look at those five rocks in my trophy case, I remember the lessons I learned that day.

I'm reminded that life isn't made of mountaintops; it's full of battles, valleys and depressions. Those may not be the words you want to hear but they're true. The good news is that if you look hard enough, in every valley (usually at the bottom) you will find a little brook. It may be small and hidden from view. You might have to search for it concealed in the grass or perhaps it's flowing just beneath the surface – but it's there! In every dark place, it's there. It runs "the length of the valley" reminding me of the His promise.

He will **NEVER LEAVE US OR FORSAKE US**.

Matthew 28:20b (KJV)

[20] ...I am with you <u>always</u>, even unto the end of the world. Amen.

David knew what he was looking for, he knew where his ammunition was hiding, because he had been there before. It was in different place, another battle, on a different day; but it was still the same. He knew that what he needed was buried beneath the waters of that brook. He had done it so many times before, and now it was time to do it again.

Just like I did three thousand years later, David dropped to his knees and began vigilantly reaching beneath the surface. He was "feeling around" for just the right rock for his fight. One by one, he pulled the stones from the creek to examine them. He rubbed them in his hands cautiously considering their size, their shape and their weight. His courage and confidence grew with every stone he grabbed as he thoughtfully selected each rock and slipped them into a small pouch. Finally as the Bible said, he had selected "five smooth stones" and put them in a Shepherd's bag.

Theologians can debate for years (as they usually do with everything) about the significance of those "smooth stones." But if you're like me, and have been in your fair share of valleys and battles, a debate isn't what you're looking for, inspiration is ...and these rocks do the trick!

Think about the analogy, that in our battle scarred existence, there's a constant source of refreshment – a "river of life!" This stream originates in the heavens and rains down to us, coming from the high places and flowing to the lowest valleys. It carries in it refreshment for your soul and spirit; and life for your survival. It isn't always clear and sometimes it can be cold and uncomfortable. But to those that are willing, to abandon their reservations and drop to their knees and reach in – they will find life and hope and strength.

I personally believe that while it's impressive to memorize countless scriptures; it won't be the verses you put in your head, but those that you put in your heart that will change your life. The Bible declares that all scripture is good for reproof, correction and instruction; and that's true. But I believe that during those times of struggle, in those dark places of confusion, and in the valley of despair we can *"feel around"* in the Word of God and find a handful scriptures that will become your powerful arsenals for a lifetime. Time and time again you will find yourself reaching deep into your heart to retrieve that favorite verse. It will shine like a beacon in the darkness. It will be a comfort in times of fear and doubt; a staff to hold you up when you're weary and a rod to defend and protect you.

The Word Is the bread of life for the hungry, water for your thirst, milk for babes and honey for dessert.

Matthew 4:4 (NIV) - *Bread*
[4] Jesus answered, "It is written: 'Man shall not live on bread alone, but on every word that comes from the mouth of God.

John 4:14 (NIV) - *Water*
[14] but whoever drinks the water I give them will never thirst. Indeed, the water I give them will become in them a spring of water welling up to eternal life."

1 Peter 2:2 (KJV) - *Milk*
[2] As newborn babes, desire the sincere milk of the word, that ye may grow thereby:

Psalm 119:103 (KJV) - *Honey*
[103] How sweet are thy words unto my taste! yea, sweeter than honey to my mouth!

Psalm 119:105 (KJV) - *Light*
[105] Thy word is a lamp unto my feet, and a light unto my path.

Psalm 23:4 (KJV) – *Comfort & Protection*
[4] Yea, though I walk through the valley of the shadow of death, I will fear no evil: for thou art with me; thy rod and thy staff they comfort me.

Now You Try...
Start digging in the Water!

Pick out 5 scriptures and commit them not just to your memory, but to your heart. Let today be a turning point in your life. Try God! Reach into the Bible (right now!) and "feel around" and find...

Your 5 Smooth Stones!
Write them down and put them in your heart.

My 1st Rock:

My 2nd Rock:

My 3rd Rock:

My 4th Rock:

My 5th Rock:

David put the stones in "A Shepherd's Bag".

To me, this has significance and denotes an item that is "special" or unique to a Shepherd. I'm also reminded of God's pleasure with those that have a *"Shepherd's Heart."*

> As you select your 5 stones of scripture,
> make sure that you put them in a
> **Shepherd's Heart.**

The Word isn't meant to be a club of retribution, but a rod of protection. It's not meant to shackle people with legalism and judgment, but to set them free through the love of the Righteous Judge. It isn't given to you for a scepter to "Lord over" others, but a staff to rescue the perishing. Take time and make a few notes about what makes a **Shepherd's Heart.**

My Notes:

Chapter 8

Put a Rock in it!

Have you ever met those people (not just in church, but everywhere) that are always ready to correct or judge someone else. Among the "religious folk" these people can whip out scriptures like a switchblade, and faster than a quick-draw cowboy. They seem to have an endless supply of verses, always for someone else, but few for themselves.

If I could draw you a picture of them, they would look like adolescent teenagers that already know everything, with little time to listen to anyone else. Their clothes are tight and bulging, because every pocket is filled to the brim - packed full of rocks. They don't have five stones, they have five hundred. They really aren't doing anything for the Kingdom of God on their own but they're anxiously waiting for the chance to throw rocks at someone else. Unlike this chapter title, you don't want them to "put a rock in it" ...you want them to *"put a sock in it!"*

The Word of God is described as a sword. It's never been described or meant to be a spear to throw at someone else. It's a sword because it's not for someone else – it's for you! It's personal.

Hebrews 4:12 (NIV)

[12] For the **word of God is alive and active**. Sharper than any double-edged sword, it penetrates even to dividing soul and spirit, joints and marrow; it judges the thoughts and attitudes of the heart.

The Word of God is indeed powerful and will work miracles in your life and family that you've never dreamed possible – I know it did for ours! But why did it say the Word is *"alive and active?"* What does that mean, and how does it work? How can paper and ink come alive and become active? The short answer is – it can't! Paper and ink alone can only provide information. But when those "words" given to us from God are **mixed with faith** – it becomes "*the Power of God*," (Ro. 1:16) and nothing is impossible. But without faith, nothing happens, and it's impossible to please God.

Hebrews 4:2 (KJV)
[2] For unto us was the gospel preached, as well as unto them: but the word preached did not profit them, not being **mixed with faith** in them that heard it.

Hebrews 11:6 (NIV)
[6] And **without faith it is impossible to please God**, because anyone who comes to him must believe that he exists and that **he rewards those who earnestly seek him.**

With four stones in the shepherd's pouch and one in his hand, David pulled out his sling. It's a strange looking object by our standards, but in those days they were quite common and used very effectively. David was comfortable with his sling because he had been using it all his life.

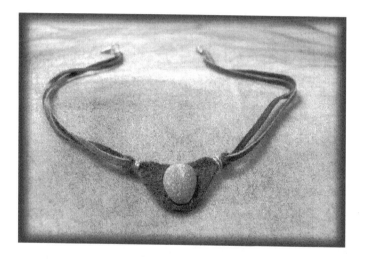

A sling has a small cradle or *pouch* in the middle of two lengths of cord. The sling stone is placed in the pouch and swung at over 6 revolutions a second. The *Slinger* releases one end at the precise moment to hurl the stone with incredible velocity. The sling and stone are still used today; in the middle east, in combat and by sportsman worldwide. The Guinness record for slinging a stone is 1,434 ft 1 in), using a 51 inch long sling and a 1.8 oz stone.

One day as I was looking at the "5 stones" sitting on the bookshelf in my office, I shifted my focus to the sling I had bought in Bethlehem. I took the sling and stones down to examine them I realized something amazing about this weapon. I was already convinced what the stones best represented to me ...they are the scriptures that I have hidden in my heart.

Psalm 119:11 (NIV)

[11] I have hidden your word in my heart
   that I might not sin against you.

BUT WOW! THEN IT HIT ME – THE SLING!

The sling is exactly like faith!
By itself, the sling is useless.
It has no power, unless it has a rock in it!

James 2:20 (KJV)
[20] But don't you know, O vain man, that faith without works is dead?

Faith alone, without works,
without the Word in the center of it,
is as worthless as a sling without a stone!

Likewise, the stones have only limited power
...and they will do little by themselves.

BUT WHEN YOU PUT A ROCK IN IT..

EVERYTHING CHANGES!

When you wrap that sling around the stone, it's no longer a rope and a rock – it's a weapon!

Likewise... when you reach into your heart and draw out one of those familiar scriptures and wrap your sling of faith around it; then it comes alive!

it's not just words ...it's a weapon!

When the Word is *"mix it with faith"* the two become one, just like the sling and stone. Another interesting thought is that unless the sling "is moving" there is nothing to hold the stone in place. The centrifugal force created by the whirling sling locks the stone in place until one end of the sling is *"released."* James 2 says that "without works" faith is dead. In other words, if your faith isn't *"on the move"* – it's dead! Unless your faith is moving, there is no power to hold the Word (or stone) in its place.

But when you've been to the valley and searched through the water to find the stones you needed and buried them in your heart; and when you courageously face your enemy and reach into the depths of your soul to grab *"that verse"* and place God's Word in the center of your faith; and when you start whirling your faith above your head in praise, trusting in the Word that it holds...

...LOOK OUT GIANT!
HERE YOU COME!

When the challenge comes (and it surely will come), and when the time is right (and you'll know when), you will run to the battle and "release your faith," and hurl the Word at supreme velocity, with pinpoint accuracy and bring down your adversary!

2 Corinthians 10:4 (NIV)
⁴ The weapons we fight with are not the weapons of the world. On the contrary, they have divine power to demolish strongholds.

Chapter 9

Run to the Battle

It's easy to get inspired and feel your faith grow when you're sitting in a church listening to your favorite speaker and worshipping with a group of your friends to the music of the praise team. And it's not hard to be motivated when a famous motivational speaker demonstrates practical life solutions to hypothetical circumstances. The problems arise when you go back home, and cold hard reality hits you in the face. You can't live your life riding the conference circuit and I doubt that the praise team will be willing to go home with you.

At some point you have to decide what kind of life you're going to live. Remember... what you put up with, you'll end up with! Are you going to be a victim or a victor?

Life.*

*Available for a limited time only. Limit one (1) per person. Subject to change without notice. Provided "as is" and without any warranties. Non transferable and is the sole responsibility of the recipient. May incur damages arising from use or misuse. Additional parts sold separately. Your mileage may vary. Subject to all applicable fees and taxes. Terms and conditions apply. Other restrictions apply.

Will you shoot for the stars or settle for the sand? How will you handle disappointment; will you just stop trying or will you be the person that gets up again and again after every defeat? Will you earn the title of Captain because you learned how to adjust your sails to ride out a storm or will you just talk and pretend while you read the latest sailing magazines in the comfort of your home?

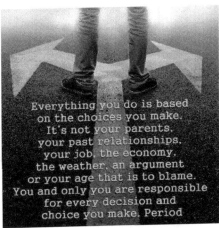

Everything you do is based on the choices you make. It's not your parents, your past relationships, your job, the economy, the weather, an argument or your age that is to blame. You and only you are responsible for every decision and choice you make. Period

By the way, this isn't a test and there are no incorrect answers. This is a choice; your choice, about your life and how you will spend it.

You can live in a cave if you want too. It's safe, secluded, and these days ...it may even come with cable TV! But it'll still be a cave ...not much of a life. To find your true happiness, purpose and destiny there will come a time when you have to face your enemies - we call them "issues" today.

David was ready! He was "chomping at the bit" for his chance to fight – he couldn't wait!

Prayer isn't just about being thankful or praying for missionaries or sick friends at church. It may include all those things, but prayer is much more. Prayer is about connecting with God in a secret place. A place where you and God commune together. Prayer's a place where you ask God to take you apart and put you back together; but with a clear vision of what He wants for your life. That's what David did in those lonely fields watching sheep. Those were the prayers that gave birth to the Psalms that flowed from David's pen. And that's why he was ready, right then, right there, he was ready for Goliath.

It's interesting that David was so pumped-up that he even inspired the fearful Israelites and Saul with some hope – but Goliath was unimpressed. The Word said: *"...and the Philistine came on."* Just because you get excited when your faith grows at Sunday morning church, doesn't mean that your enemy is going anywhere. He'll be waiting for you, right there on Monday.

As soon as David showed his face, Goliath heckled him with cursing and laughter. And once again David was haunted by the label that he hated most. He father had said it, his brothers said it, the soldiers said it, the leaders said it, King Saul said it – and now his enemy was saying it – *YOU'RE JUST A KID!* "...I will rip you apart and give your flesh to the birds and the beasts."

David was SICK of being called a kid, but he never became defensive. Instead, he rebuked Goliath and laughed while he informed him that he had brought the wrong weapons. Goliath had come with a sword, a spear and a shield and screaming about what "he was going to do." David never defended his age or explained his inexperience. He didn't mention the sling in his hand or the stones in his pocket ...but he did reveal a secret!

It was the same secret that authorized Moses to stand before Pharaoh and set the people free. It was the same secret that caused Gideon to finally step away from hiding in the winepress and gave Peter the courage to step out of the boat and onto the open sea. In fact it's the same secret that empowered every great miracle in the Bible and

...it's still valid to all of us today.

I Samuel 17:45 David said:

"**45** David said to the Philistine, "You come against me with sword and spear and javelin, but ***I come against you in the name of the Lord Almighty***, the God of the armies of Israel, whom you have defied. **46** This day ***the Lord will deliver you into my hands***, and I'll strike you down and cut off your head.

The **SECRET** was:

David <u>KNEW</u> that the Lord was with him! That's what allowed him to say what he said. Just as God told Moses that the **"I AM"** had sent him; or when the *"Angel"* told Gideon to go in **"this thy might,"** **"that the Lord had sent him";** or when Peter asked Jesus, "<u>*if it's you*</u>, bid me to come to you **...and the Lord said COME.**

David wasn't guessing and he wasn't hoping; **he <u>KNEW</u> that the Lord was with him.**

> **That's the secret!**
> **It always has been and always will be...**
> **and YOU can know it too.**

But how? How can you know that the Lord is with you and be sure that He'll deliver you? There're two answers – one is personal and the other is purpose.

The 1st answer is personal. Everything God does is ultimately about relationship. You and I were created for God's pleasure because He desires relationship. Jesus redeems us that we might have a relationship with Him. There's seldom any "lightning bolts" from heaven for confirmation. God "spoke" to Moses. The Angel "spoke" to Gideon, and it was to a foggy figure in the dark that Peter asked "if it's you Jesus," that "spoke back" and said "come".

David had spent years in prayer both morning and evening and he "knew" God. The Word of God says, "my sheep hear my voice and they know me." God desires that same relationship with you. And when you spend enough time in the presence of God in worship and prayer it will become personal for you too. Then YOU will begin to hear His Voice and you will KNOW Him. ...and you'll **_know_** when it's Him speaking to you!

The 2nd answer is purpose. With man, most things are all about pleasure; but with God everything is about purpose. Everything God does has purpose. If you want to know if God is leading you – look for the purpose, if there is one. With God, it's all about His purpose. When David scolded Goliath, he told him that God would deliver him... **_"that all the earth may know that there is a God in Israel."_** "...and the assembly will know that the Lord doesn't save by the sword and spear; for the battle is the Lords!...

That's purpose!

When David finished speaking...
He Ran to the Battle!

One version interpreted it...
"David ran swiftly, like a charging Lion!"

When you discover how pray and worship, as you seek to know Him in a personal way; and when you surrender your desires for His; and when you commit your ways to Him - for His purpose...

THEN YOU"LL KNOW!

You won't need to surf from conference to conference or hang onto every song and sermon.

You won't need a motivational speaker to walk you through the minefields of this life.

The troubles in this life won't shock you and the threats of the enemy won't scare you.

Instead you will boldly declare...

The Lord will deliver me!

and YOU will...

Run swiftly like a charging Lion!

Terry W. Bomar

Chapter 10

Tips from the Taxidermist

He cringed every time he heard it, but It was true
...David was *"just a kid."* He was a young, thin, good
looking boy in his teens that had a heart that
burned for God. He may have been born with his
good looks and body frame, but his faith and spirit
was chiseled out by a thousand choices. When he
struggled with insecurity and isolation; he made a
choice. When he felt abandoned and ignored; he
made a choice. When he was overcome with
loneliness and fear; he made a choice. When he

grappled with confusion and doubt; he made a choice. He overcame feelings of jealousy and resentment, with a choice. He responded to disappointments and pain with a choice. With every crushing blow from life's hammer of unfairness, he chipped away at his carnality and drew closer to God. The emotional forces that attempted to destroy him, instead meticulously sculpted his character and fashioned his heart after God. David slogged from the shadows of obscurity onto the greatest stage of human history. He grew with every throbbing step from faith …to faith, and watched his hardships become a platform for greatness.

His day had finally come; adrenaline was coursing through his body as he a shouted the victory cry and ran toward Goliath. He left the doubters and critics behind, whirling his loaded sling high in the air, he charged across the valley floor toward his colossal foe. Goliath, the master warrior, positioned himself for the kill, but he never imagined that he would be the one to die. David advanced like a sprinting lion with his eyes fixed on the enemy. Suddenly the sound of the sling beating the air went silent when the kid released the stone toward his target. Goliath never saw it coming… and he didn't make a sound. Only the thud of his cracking skull was heard an instant before the titan staggered and collapsed into a crumpled heap in the grass.

David "the kid" was a hero!

I wonder how often we fail to recognize how much we've grown because of the hardships we've overcome. Do we really understand that it's only through larger challenges that we test our limits and birth our gifts and talents? My mother faced a terrible time with me and suffered a thousand sleepless nights. She was tormented by the forces that were controlling her "little man." She tried everything she could but nothing seemed to work. All she had left was God, but...

when all you have left is God
...you have it ALL!

She turned to God completely and unconditionally. There were no great revelations, and no sign that God had heard her prayers or if He even cared; but she knew that God was leading her. She didn't realize it while confronting me in my bedroom that night, but that was the turning point in our lives. She did know that she had touched God ...and she wanted more.

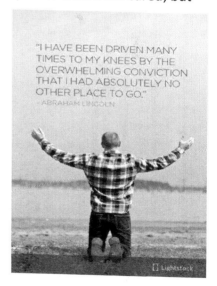

"I HAVE BEEN DRIVEN MANY TIMES TO MY KNEES BY THE OVERWHELMING CONVICTION THAT I HAD ABSOLUTELY NO OTHER PLACE TO GO."
- ABRAHAM LINCOLN

Lightstock

From that night on she was totally different. She boldly told me that she had released me into God's hands and turned me over to Him. She never "preached at me" again, but often she would plant a tiny seed of faith in me. She stopped talking about what I was doing wrong and started dropping tidbits of what she believed God had planned for me. She stopped running away from the "giant problem" I had become and started running toward her son, that she was determined to save.

God used David's singular battle with Goliath to stop the Philistine army in its tracks He stopped them from assaulting the major cities in the heart of Israel. When you're locked in your own personal conflict, the fog of war can cloud your judgment and perspective. In the chaos, it's easy to forget that God has a plan for you and your family. But the battle that you're in today may be protecting the very heart of God's purpose for your life and those you love.

When David's giant hit the ground... the battle was over, but the job wasn't finished. The enemy was unconscious, but he wasn't dead. David rushed over and grabbed the huge sword... and with one violent blow he finished him off. He severed his neck and lifted the head of Goliath up for all the world to see!

It must have been a gruesome sight as the bloody head of the most feared man in the world dangled from the hand of David. The blood dripped and pooled at David's feet while he waived his prize at the cheering armies that were now in hot pursuit of the fleeing Philistines. David had no plans to take his trophy to the taxidermist, or hang Goliath's head in his "man-cave;" but he did want to show the King. The Bible reports that Abner brought David before the King *"with the head of the Philistine in his hand."* As he stood before King Saul with the bloody dripping head in his hand, the King only had one burning question: ***"Who are you?"***

Trophies are very important. The severed head of their champion in the hands of "that kid" struck tremendous fear in the heart of the Philistines. But when David raised it high in the air, the hearts of all Israel where inspired and encouraged. It's recorded that David took the head to Jerusalem and he took Goliath's weapons and armor to his own tent. Trophies are designed for glory; to be memorials reminding you of victorious achievements and success. They should be constant reminders of who you are, what you've done; and what you **CAN** do! Trophies should be memorials of "mountain tops" in your life, that you can climb again and again to recall the magnificent view. But, trophies cannot and should never *"be your life."* If you choose to live for the mountain tops or just for the prizes you can collect, your life will become shallow. You will eventually sell your character, your purpose and your happiness ...all for the next fleeting prize. Your life trophies must be supported by your character or they will corrode in vain conceit. To enjoy an authentic life full of confidence and honor you must not be defined by superficial rewards, but by your excellence; your ethics; and your enemies. The head of Goliath and the freedom of Israel were the result of David's authentic life. With or without the trophies - David was real. David's character and courage prepared him for greatness. And if it had been David's lifeless body lying in the field when the sun went down; his last valiant breath would not have been in vain because... ***David was real!***

David was a man of excellence whether he was feeding sheep or fighting Philistines. He was a man of ethics whether it cost him his career or cost him his life. And David will forever be defined not by the kingdom he built ...but by the enemy he beat! From that day forward, David's name would forever be linked to the enemy he defeated. It was that one battle that launched his fame into immortality.

The King asked David, "Who are you?
Now... it's your turn to answer same question:

Who are You?

What are your priorities?
What's more important to you?
WHERE you are ...or WHO you are?

What defines who you are today?
What standards do you use to govern your life?
What are the ethics that shape your character?
What enemies have you overcome?

ALL THESE...
are things that you can determine today!

Now answer the question:
Where are You?

You may be facing the toughest times of your life right now. Your enemy may appear to be a giant towering over you and threatening the very heart of your life. But you don't have to give in or give up. The battle you're facing may be your launching pad.

You may be thinking that you've been forgotten, overlooked and doomed to the same valley you've been stuck in for years.

SOMETIMES GOD DOESN'T CHANGE YOUR SITUATION BECAUSE HE'S TRYING TO CHANGE YOUR HEART.

You may have thought that God doesn't hear you ...or worse, that He doesn't care ...but you're wrong!

When God doesn't move the Giant (obstacle) it's because He wants to meet you in the valley - to discover your strengths.

And if you're still stuck in a valley ...maybe it's because there is still a giant you need to kill.

Never forget... the world thinks that the story of "David and Goliath" was the ultimate metaphor for the improbable, and that David was the under-dog because "all he had" was a sling and stone, but...

A sling and stone was ALL he needed!

Don't be afraid of Giants!

The society we live in are masters at building "dreadful giants" for us to fear. They have enormous PR firms spending millions of dollars every day to make us afraid of everything you can imagine. They peddle fear so they can sell you "their protection." The world system (Jesus called "mammon"), two significant "laws." One is the law of *"supply and demand,"* and the other is the law of *"fear and shortage."* If you want it ...they will sell it to you. If a lot of you want it ...they'll sell it to you, for more. If they can make you afraid of something ...they can sell you the fix for it. If they can make you think that you "need" something, and it's running out ...they can gouge the price.

God's law is just the opposite, it's one of...
"Faith and Abundance,"
because His ways are higher than our ways.

Isaiah 55:9 (NIV)
9 "As the heavens are higher than the earth,
so are my ways higher than your ways
and my thoughts than your thoughts.

God gives you the gift of free-will and invites you to trust and follow Him by faith. The "world" tries to bluff you with "phony giants," and intimidate you into submission. They fabricate giants of every shape, size and material and then convince you that you're powerless to defeat them!

They have conceived "labels" of every description to destroy your strength and self-confidence; in order to beguile you into serving them. The world system pounds their message into your mind from countless media sources, celebrities, the internet, and of course the all-knowing "experts." They preach that you're so weak that you're powerless without their products and services. You can't raise your kids without their guidance, you can't quit smoking without a patch, you can't diet without a pill, and of course if you're an alcoholic or addict you can never be healed – only recover – with their constant help of course.

Should you dare to believe anything different, they have labels for you too – you're ignorant, naïve, foolish, or a religious nut, etc. It sounds like what they said to David doesn't it... *"you're just a kid!"*

Believe what you choose, but here's just a sample of what God says about you:

1 John 4:4 (NIV)

[4] You, dear children, are from God and have overcome them, because the one who is in you is greater than the one who is in the world.

Philippians 4:6-7 (NIV)
[6] Do not be anxious about anything, but in every situation, by prayer and petition, with thanksgiving, present your requests to God. [7] And the peace of God, which transcends all understanding, will guard your hearts and your minds in Christ Jesus.

2 Corinthians 10:3-5 (NIV)
[3] For though we live in the world, we do not wage war as the world does. [4] The weapons we fight with are not the weapons of the world. On the contrary, they have divine power to

demolish strongholds. **5** We demolish arguments and every pretension that sets itself up against the knowledge of God, and we take captive every thought to make it obedient to Christ.

1 Peter 2:9-10 (NIV)

9 But you are a chosen people, a royal priesthood, a holy nation, God's special possession, that you may declare the praises of him who called you out of darkness into his wonderful light. **10** Once you were not a people, but now you are the people of God; once you had not received mercy, but now you have received mercy.

Luke 18:27 (KJV)

27 And he said, The things which are impossible with men are possible with God.

Ephesians 3:19-21 (KJV)

19 And to know the love of Christ, which passeth knowledge, that ye might be filled with all the fullness of God. **20** Now unto him that is able to do exceeding abundantly above all that we ask or think, according to the power that worketh in us, **21** Unto him be glory in the church by Christ Jesus throughout all ages, world without end. Amen.

Read those verses and remember... that it doesn't matter if it's your child, your relationship, your career or any other *"giant"* –

**your problems may be smaller than you think –
and YOU are bigger than you thought!**

Researchers studied Goliath to determine why he grew to 13'4". Most of the studies claim that he had *"Gigantism or Acromegaly."* There have been many throughout history who've had the disease, most notably, André Roussimoff (7' 4") better known as *"Andre the Giant;" and* Robert Wadlow (8'11") *"the Tallest Man in the World."* Some believe that Abraham Lincoln may have had it which explained why he was so tall. The disease is caused by a benign tumor effecting the pituitary gland, and besides causing the person to grow large and tall, other noticeable symptoms are vision problems such as "near-sightedness" or double-vision, sometimes slow reflexes, among others.

One study pointed out that each time Goliath appeared he was preceded (or perhaps led) by a shield-bearer; and each time Goliath called for Israel to send down a warrior he said "let us fight." The study asserts that Goliath said that because of the "single combat" tradition and Goliath wanted the man to "come down to him, and fight one to one." The study then posed an interesting question, why did Goliath say: "come to me?"

He most likely said the same thing every time he challenged them, and it's recorded twice in scripture. He said it once to Israel and again to David directly ...even as David approached him. Then the study pointed out the oddest comment Goliath made during the entire exchange.

> **I Samuel 17:43-44** (NIV)
> [43] He said to David, "**Am I a dog, that you come at me with <u>sticks?</u>**" And the Philistine cursed David by his gods. [44] "Come to me," he said, "and I'll give your flesh to the birds and the wild animals!"

If Goliath had *"Acromegaly"* it would explain it all. If the disease caused vision problems, it quite possible that He would've been preceded (or led) because he needed help. Battle historians say that Goliath was slow and "lumbering" which is common among those with *Acromegaly* .

Goliath was prepared to fight, but fight his way. For *heavy infantrymen* like Goliath, size and strength was the advantage and speed wasn't needed. But why did he say "come to me" – twice! Heavy infantry were trained to fight in close proximity; but. if he had poor vision, he needed to draw his opponent close to him rather than chase after them.

And if he had "double vision," that would explain why Goliath said:
"**Am I a dog, that you come at me with <u>sticks?</u>**"

David only carried his staff (one stick), but Goliath said **"sticks"** – more than one stick!

If he was "near-sighted" (as many with the disease are) it explains why when David immediately started sprinting towards him, Goliath did nothing – yes, because he was slow and maybe because...
he couldn't see him at that distance!

Maybe David wasn't the "underdog" at all.

David was a young quick kid, that was experienced with a sling. *"Slingers"* were part of the *Artillery Branch* along with the *Archers*. They moved with great swiftness and struck from a distance! Goliath was a lumbering, heavy infantryman, expecting a sword fight and wearing over 100lbs of armor; he was no match for the blazing speed of David. Maybe the Philistines marched Goliath out because his massive size was intimidating all by itself; and if anyone dared to challenge him "on his terms" at close quarters – he would destroy them!

But David had no intention of abandoning his skills with the sling to fight Goliath as infantry; and you should do the same! You don't have to wrestle in hand-to-hand combat - you can strike from a distance! The battle is the Lord's and He's given you the Word; and the faith that makes it alive!

Think about it! If you follow the Lord, then He has given you His Word. (*THE **STONES!***)

Hebrews 4:12a (KJV)
12 For the word of God is _**quick**_, and _**powerful,**_ and *sharper than any two-edged sword...*

It's QUICK and Powerful... and when it's MIXED with FAITH *(THE **SLING!**)*

1 Peter 1:5 (KJV)
"**5** Who *are kept by the power of God <u>through faith</u> unto salvation...*"

*IT IS **POWER** OF OUR SALVATION!*

The next time you find yourself facing extraordinary opposition that tempts to run away – STOP!

You need <u>this</u> much faith!

Before you panic when you're in the fight of your life, think about **WHO** is on your side. When you look up and some "phony giant" marches out taunting you into depression, take a closer look. Consider that Goliath's massive size, the very thing that was the source of his apparent strength ...was also the source of his greatest weakness.

And Remember...

NEVER BE AFRAID OF GIANTS!
because they're <u>never</u>
as powerful as they seem.

And...

YOU
HAVE A SLING IN YOUR POCKET!

What about Mom?

The rest of a personal story...

You already know how David's battle ended that day; but what about my mother and the *little monster* she was facing – how did that turn out?

It's true that Mom went to church *"all the time,"* but that night was different and she was different, because... she touched God!

and... God touched her too!

She must have received the *spirit of David* that night because she acted just like him. She was ablaze with passion for God's promises and she wasn't about to let Satan have her son! She kicked open my bedroom door and declared that she belonged to God and she'd turned me over to Him – and she did!

With that, she spun around and left the room as quickly as she had entered. At first I thought... great! I will do anything I please. But a few minutes later as I sat in the silence, I felt a strange sense of loneliness. I knew that the best friend I had - had just cut me loose.

In the days that followed my mother no longer approached me like heavy infantry in hand to hand combat - trying to control my outrageous behavior.

Instead she moved with the speed and spirit of David, striking with her sling and stone from a distance! She never *"preached at me,"* and never tried to correct or punish me. Instead she started bombarding heaven with a barrage of prayers – not in desperation but with faith that God was going to turn me around – she knew it!

Then she started reaching into the water of the Word and pulled out verses of faith and courage that God would do the things that were impossible. She buried those words of faith and courage in her shepherd's heart and started looking for me. She didn't *"quote me scriptures,"* she learned them herself and extracted their wisdom and loaded up her sling. She never marched around with "churchy clichés" or threats of damnation and doom. Instead she moved as swift as a "slinger" and would dart in to where I would be sitting and hit me with a seed of faith - like a stone!

In thirty seconds she could hurl a single statement and dart out again, before I knew what hit me! I never saw it coming!

One day I was just watching TV… and Wham! She struck me with: "God has something great planned for you," and she was gone before I could argue. A few days later I was working of some speakers for my car… and Smack! She hit me with a glancing blow: "One day… you're gonna be working on sermons as hard as you're working on those speakers!" Before I realized what she said… she was gone again. And the day I told her that was leaving for a weekend trip to Nashville with my friends; I fully expected a fight, but what I got was… Blam! "Have a good time, but one of these days you're gonna be taking trips to preach – maybe as a missionary." I shook my head in disgust and said: "She must really be crazy!"

But Mom just blew the smoke off her sling… and slipped it back into her purse with a smile.

It didn't take too many weeks for those seeds to sprout; and God was adding the rain. I started to wonder why I was fighting God so hard? What "IF" God had something better for me? Faith was starting to grow inside and storms were raging on the outside. Soon David (oops, I mean Mom) would sling it the final blow… from a distance!

It was 2 a.m. the day after Thanksgiving. Mother had no idea where I was or if I was coming home at all. She had gone to bed early after cooking all day for Thanksgiving. I had been midnight bowling with my brother and his wife and we were on the way home, when they started in on me about becoming a Christian. I responded just like you would expect a giant to respond – I started cursing at them. I let them know that I wanted nothing to do with their church, their Bibles, or their Jesus! I hurled a few insults for added protection – and insisted that churches were full of hypocrites and money grubbing preachers. I demanded that they keep their opinions to themselves because I was happy doing drugs, and I didn't need them.

They backed off and after an awkward ride home, we pulled in the driveway a little before 3 a.m. Then they asked, if they could ask me one question. It stopped me in my tracks because they didn't know the thoughts God had been pouring through my head for weeks. They asked: "Terry, you've tried everything from Boones Farm to Cocaine – why don't you try God? Why're you fighting against Him? What have you got to lose? Those words were exactly what God had been pelting me with for weeks – every time mom would dropped one of those positive seeds (stones) of hers. I didn't say a word and listened as my brother read me two scriptures.

Psalm 34:8 (NIV)
8 Taste and see that the Lord is good;

Psalm 37:4 (KJV)
4 Delight thyself also in the Lord: and he shall give thee the desires of thine heart.

Twenty minutes before, I was cursing at them – now I was listening. My brother challenged me to *"just try it."* He added, *"if I offered you drugs, you would try that – why not try this? The other verse says that God will give you the desires of your heart, what have you got to lose? Just try it?"*

So I looked at my watch – it was 3 a.m. on Nov 29th., when I prayed and told God that I was going to try Him *"for two-weeks;"* and *"if it didn't work for me like it did those guys in the Bible... I was going back to drugs!"* It worked! I was never... ever... the same! After ten minutes of praying and ten minutes of talking, I slipped quietly into the house for bed.

But what about mom? Well that's the really cool part of the story! Since the night she turned me over to God, she prayed to Him for a miracle and kept slinging words of faith at me. So God surely wasn't going to leave her out this miracle night.

I woke up excited the next morning and ran to tell mom what just happened the night before; but she stopped me in the hall. She blurted out... *"You're not going believe what happened last night!"* *"Mom! Wait!"* *"What I've got to tell you is much better!"* She insisted, so I let her go first. She said: *"Terry... Last night, I was in a dead sleep and God woke me wide awake and told me to pray for my youngest son. So Terry, I looked at the clock and got on my knees by the bed and prayed for you at three o'clock in the morning!"*

I started to cry when she said she looked at the clock and it was 3 a.m. because...

I knew that God did that "for her... not me!"

He gave her a miraculous confirmation
that He had heard her prayer.

God woke her up at just in time for the fight. Mom grabbed her sling and stones and slipped down beside the bed. She didn't know that I was right outside when she started swinging her faith around; but when she let it go...

***the stone killed a Giant in the driveway
and she rescued her "Little Man"
right out of the mouth of the Lion!***

and she was right...

***God did have a big plan
for me.***

ABOUT THE AUTHOR

Award-winning Speaker, Minister, Author, Screenwriter and Adventurer

Terry grew up in Memphis, Tenn. and entered the ministry as a very young man. His experience as a speaker, writer, pastor and adventurer has carried him all over the world. He has pastored churches in Tennessee, Hawaii and Florida; and the Caribbean. He has been a missionary serving third-world countries and a Chaplin in County, State and Federal Prisons. He was voted one of the top 25 ministers in America and received an invitation to the U.S. Presidential Inauguration in honor of his work.

In 1992 he founded Young Adventurers, children's charity and began working with celebrity spokespersons which led to his close personal friendship with Dan Haggerty. For over 15 years Terry has worked with Dan in faith and family film projects. But, Terry's first priority is his family, his ministry and his charity work. Terry's knowledge of the Word and insight into human nature and made him a fascinating story-teller, motivational speaker and leader. His international experiences have made him a sought after speaker for churches and conferences around the world.

I want to thank Sarah for her dedication to the Lord and love for people. I want to share with you the gift she sent to me of the song she wrote....

JUST ONE SMOOTH STONE

Just one smooth stone,
That's all it took!
Just one smooth stone
Out of the brook.
Just one smooth stone
Brought down Goliath.
Just one smooth stone
Saves he who crieth!

Just one smooth stone,
A promise heard.
Just one smooth stone
From God's own word.
Just one smooth stone
Everywhere you go;
Just one smooth stone
Fells every foe!

By: Sarah Pinkerton Frase

Contact Information:

Terry W. Bomar
Palm Beach, Florida
Twbomar@aol.com

www.TerryBomar.com

More Titles in the
New Life "By the Book" Series

From the Cave to the Crown
Gideon's Victory Over Depression

Footsteps of the Shepherd
A magnificent journey through the 23rd Psalm

Made in the USA
Charleston, SC
25 March 2016